Thank you very much for reading this book.

Title: Beyond the Deed: Exploring the Dark Side of Blockchain for Land Ownership

Subtitle: Assessing Risks and Promoting Responsible Implementation

Author: Herman Strange

Table of Contents

Introduction
Explanation of blockchain technology for land ownership documentation

Blockchain technology is a distributed, decentralized ledger system that allows for secure, transparent and immutable record-keeping of transactions. This technology has been identified as a possible solution to problems with traditional land registration systems, which can be slow, costly, and prone to corruption and errors.

Blockchain technology can be used for land ownership documentation by creating a tamper-proof, digital record of all property transactions. This can help to improve transparency, reduce fraud, and provide an accessible and trustworthy source of information on land ownership.

At its core, a blockchain is a decentralized, distributed database that allows multiple parties to access and update records in a secure and transparent way. Every transaction on the blockchain is verified by a network of computers, known as nodes, before being added to the ledger. Once added, the transaction is immutable, meaning that it cannot be altered or deleted without the consensus of the network.

The security of the blockchain is maintained through a combination of cryptography, consensus algorithms, and economic incentives. Cryptography is used to protect the integrity of the data, while consensus algorithms ensure that all nodes on the network agree on the validity of each transaction. Economic incentives, such as rewards for maintaining the network or penalties for bad behavior, help to ensure that participants act in the best interest of the network as a whole.

In the context of land ownership documentation, a blockchain can be used to create a digital record of each property transaction, including the sale, purchase, transfer, or lease of land. Each transaction would be recorded on the blockchain as a block, which would include information such as the parties involved, the date and time of the transaction, and the terms of the agreement.

This digital record could then be accessed by anyone with permission to view it, including government agencies, property owners, and interested parties. The use of blockchain technology could help to reduce the risk of fraud and corruption in land ownership documentation, while also increasing transparency and accessibility.

However, it's important to note that blockchain technology is not a panacea and does have its limitations. While it can help to solve some of the problems with traditional land registration systems, it also comes with its own set of challenges and potential risks. These risks and limitations will be discussed in further detail in the following chapters.

Importance of land ownership documentation

Land ownership documentation is essential for establishing legal ownership of a property and protecting the rights of the owner. Without proper documentation, disputes can arise, and the rightful owner may be deprived of their property.

In many countries, land ownership is an important aspect of economic growth and development. Secure and well-documented land ownership systems can promote investment, reduce poverty, and support sustainable development.

However, in many parts of the world, land ownership documentation is inadequate or non-existent. This can be due to a variety of factors, including weak governance, ineffective land administration systems, and corruption. The lack of reliable land ownership documentation can have serious consequences, including displacement of communities, loss of livelihoods, and conflict over land.

For example, in some areas, land grabbing by powerful individuals or corporations has led to forced evictions of local communities and destruction of their homes and livelihoods. Without proper documentation to prove ownership, these communities are vulnerable to losing their land and being left with nowhere to go.

In other cases, the lack of clear land ownership documentation has resulted in long-standing disputes and conflicts over land rights. These disputes can be time-consuming, costly, and can result in violence and instability in the affected communities.

Given the importance of land ownership documentation, the use of blockchain technology has been proposed as a potential solution to these problems. By creating a secure and transparent system for documenting land ownership, blockchain could help to reduce fraud, increase transparency, and promote equitable access to land.

In the following chapters, we will explore the potential benefits and risks of using blockchain for land ownership documentation, as well as the challenges that need to be addressed in the implementation of such a system.

Benefits of using blockchain

Blockchain technology has gained a lot of attention in recent years, with its potential applications in various industries. In the context of land ownership documentation, blockchain has several potential benefits that could make it a valuable tool in addressing the challenges of existing land registration systems.

1. Transparency and immutability: One of the most significant benefits of blockchain is its ability to create an immutable and transparent ledger of transactions. In the context of land ownership, this means that ownership records would be publicly accessible, and any changes or updates to the records would be recorded and verified by multiple parties, making it more challenging to manipulate or falsify data.

2. Security: Another advantage of blockchain technology is its security. The decentralized nature of blockchain means that there is no central point of control, making it more difficult for hackers or malicious actors to tamper with data. The use of cryptographic techniques in blockchain also adds another layer of security, ensuring that only authorized parties have access to the data.

3. Efficiency: Blockchain technology can also improve the efficiency of land registration systems by reducing the

time and costs associated with manual paperwork and bureaucracy. The use of smart contracts can automate many of the processes involved in land registration, reducing the need for intermediaries and minimizing the potential for errors or disputes.

4. Inclusivity: By creating a transparent and accessible system for recording land ownership, blockchain can help to promote inclusivity and provide access to land ownership documentation to a wider range of individuals and communities. This could be particularly valuable in areas where land ownership rights are not well established, and people may face barriers to accessing traditional land registration systems.

5. Reduced corruption: Another potential benefit of using blockchain for land ownership documentation is the reduced potential for corruption. The transparency and immutability of the blockchain ledger make it more challenging for corrupt individuals or organizations to manipulate or falsify data, reducing the potential for unfair distribution of land ownership.

In the following chapters, we will explore each of these benefits in more detail and examine the potential risks and challenges associated with using blockchain for land ownership documentation.

Overview of potential risks

While blockchain technology offers several potential benefits for land ownership documentation, there are also significant risks and challenges associated with its implementation. It is essential to consider these potential risks carefully and develop strategies to address them in any blockchain-based land registration system.

1. Vulnerability to fraud and manipulation: One of the primary risks associated with using blockchain for land ownership documentation is the potential for fraud and manipulation. If the blockchain system used to record land ownership is not secure, it could be vulnerable to hackers who could alter or delete records, resulting in ownership disputes and legal battles. It is crucial to ensure that appropriate security measures are in place to prevent such vulnerabilities.

2. Corruption and unfair distribution: Another potential issue is the potential for corruption in the land registration process. If a corrupt government or land registry system is in place, it could manipulate the records to benefit certain individuals or organizations, leading to unfair land ownership distribution. It is essential to ensure that the blockchain-based land registration system is designed in a

way that is transparent and reduces the potential for corruption.

3. Exclusion and marginalization: There is also the possibility that using blockchain for land ownership documentation could result in exclusion and marginalization of certain groups, such as those who do not have access to the technology or who are not familiar with how to use it. It is essential to ensure that the blockchain-based land registration system is accessible to all and that appropriate training and support are provided to those who need it.

4. Privacy concerns: Finally, there is the issue of privacy. While blockchain is designed to be secure and immutable, there is still the potential for sensitive personal information to be revealed if it is included in the blockchain records. This could potentially lead to identity theft or other forms of privacy violations. It is crucial to ensure that appropriate measures are in place to protect personal information and that privacy concerns are taken into account in the design of any blockchain-based land registration system.

In the following chapters, we will explore each of these potential risks in more detail and examine strategies for addressing them in the implementation of any blockchain-based land registration system.

Chapter 1: Fraud and Manipulation
Vulnerability to fraud and manipulation

One of the primary risks associated with using blockchain for land ownership documentation is the potential for fraud and manipulation. Blockchain-based land registration systems could be vulnerable to hacking, cyberattacks, and other forms of digital fraud that could result in tampering with or deleting records, leading to ownership disputes and legal battles.

There are several ways in which a blockchain-based land registration system could be vulnerable to fraud and manipulation. For example, if the blockchain is not designed with appropriate security measures, it could be hacked, resulting in the alteration or deletion of records. A hacker could also steal the private keys that are used to access the blockchain, enabling them to make unauthorized changes to the records.

Another potential vulnerability is the use of smart contracts in the blockchain. Smart contracts are self-executing contracts that are coded into the blockchain and automatically execute when certain conditions are met. If a smart contract is not designed correctly or has vulnerabilities in its code, it could be exploited by attackers to manipulate the records or steal information.

There is also the risk of collusion and corruption in the land registration process. For example, a corrupt government or land registry system could manipulate the records to benefit certain individuals or organizations, leading to unfair land ownership distribution. In this case, a blockchain-based land registration system could be hacked or manipulated by corrupt officials to alter the records in their favor.

To mitigate the risk of fraud and manipulation in a blockchain-based land registration system, it is essential to implement appropriate security measures. These measures could include strong encryption, multi-factor authentication, and secure key management. It is also crucial to ensure that the blockchain is designed to be transparent and immutable, making it difficult for attackers to alter or delete records.

Another way to mitigate the risk of fraud and manipulation is to conduct regular security audits and penetration testing of the blockchain-based land registration system. This can help identify vulnerabilities and weaknesses in the system, allowing developers to address them before they are exploited by attackers.

Finally, it is essential to ensure that all parties involved in the land registration process are aware of the risks of fraud and manipulation and are trained in best practices for securing their access to the blockchain-based system. This could include training on how to recognize and prevent phishing attacks, secure password management, and the safe storage of private keys. By taking these steps, the risk of fraud and manipulation in a blockchain-based land registration system can be significantly reduced.

Consequences of altered or deleted records

One of the main risks associated with using blockchain for land ownership documentation is the potential for altered or deleted records due to fraud or manipulation. This can have severe consequences for landowners, governments, and society as a whole. In this section, we will discuss some of the potential consequences of altered or deleted records in a blockchain-based land registration system.

Ownership Disputes

Altered or deleted records can lead to ownership disputes between different parties, such as landowners, government agencies, and private companies. In a blockchain-based land registration system, the immutability of the blockchain is one of its key features. If this immutability is compromised, it can undermine the trust and reliability of the system, leading to disputes and legal battles over ownership rights.

For example, if a hacker gains access to the blockchain and alters the ownership records of a particular property, this could lead to a dispute between the original owner and the new owner listed on the blockchain. If the issue is not resolved quickly and accurately, it could result in costly legal battles and cause significant harm to the parties involved.

Financial Losses

Altered or deleted records can also result in financial losses for landowners and other parties involved in the land registration process. For example, if a landowner's property is fraudulently sold to another party through manipulation of the blockchain, the original owner could suffer a significant financial loss. Similarly, if a government agency or private company's ownership rights are compromised, they could suffer significant financial losses as well.

The consequences of financial losses due to altered or deleted records can be severe, especially in developing countries where land ownership is often the primary source of wealth for many people. In these cases, financial losses could result in poverty and a lack of access to basic necessities such as food and shelter.

Social Unrest

Altered or deleted records in a blockchain-based land registration system can also lead to social unrest and political instability. For example, if a government agency is accused of manipulating the records to benefit certain individuals or organizations, this could lead to protests and civil unrest. In extreme cases, it could even lead to a government overthrow or civil war.

The potential consequences of altered or deleted records in a blockchain-based land registration system are significant and far-reaching. It is therefore essential to implement appropriate security measures and safeguards to ensure that the records are secure and immutable. These measures could include regular security audits, penetration testing, and appropriate encryption and access control protocols. By taking these steps, the risks associated with altered or deleted records can be significantly reduced.

Ownership disputes and legal battles

Ownership disputes and legal battles can arise as a result of fraudulent or manipulated land ownership records on a blockchain system. Such disputes can be costly, time-consuming, and potentially damaging to the parties involved. In this section, we will explore the potential consequences of ownership disputes and legal battles resulting from fraud and manipulation of blockchain land ownership records.

One of the primary concerns with ownership disputes is that they can result in uncertainty and instability in the land market. If there is no clear ownership title for a particular piece of land, potential buyers and lenders may be hesitant to invest in or develop it. This can have significant economic impacts on the region where the land is located, including reduced investment, job creation, and economic growth.

In addition to economic impacts, ownership disputes can also have social and environmental consequences. For example, if land is left undeveloped due to ownership disputes, it may become neglected and fall into disrepair, resulting in blight and potential health hazards for neighboring communities. On the other hand, if multiple parties are attempting to develop the same land, this can lead to environmental degradation and conflicts over resource use.

Legal battles resulting from ownership disputes can also be financially and emotionally draining for the parties involved. In some cases, such battles can go on for years, costing the parties thousands of dollars in legal fees and other expenses. Furthermore, legal battles can be emotionally taxing and may lead to increased stress, anxiety, and other negative health outcomes for the parties involved.

It is important to note that ownership disputes and legal battles are not unique to blockchain-based land ownership systems. However, the potential for fraud and manipulation of blockchain records may exacerbate these issues and make them more difficult to resolve. It is therefore critical that blockchain-based land ownership systems be designed with robust security features and rigorous auditing protocols to minimize the risk of fraudulent and manipulated records.

Smart contracts for risk mitigation

One potential way to mitigate the risk of fraud and manipulation in blockchain-based land ownership systems is through the use of smart contracts. Smart contracts are self-executing contracts with the terms of the agreement between buyer and seller being directly written into code. This allows for the automation of the contract's execution, as well as the ability to verify and enforce the terms of the contract through a blockchain network.

In the context of land ownership documentation, smart contracts can be used to automate various aspects of the land ownership transfer process, including the transfer of ownership titles, the payment of fees, and the verification of property details. This can help reduce the risk of fraud and manipulation by ensuring that ownership transfers are executed correctly and transparently.

One of the key benefits of smart contracts is that they can be programmed to include various conditions that must be met before the contract is executed. For example, a smart contract could include a requirement for the payment of a certain fee before a land ownership transfer can be executed. This would help ensure that all parties involved in the transaction are fulfilling their obligations and that the transfer is executed fairly.

Smart contracts can also be designed to include various checks and balances that help ensure the accuracy of the information included in the blockchain records. For example, a smart contract could be designed to require the verification of a land survey before a land ownership transfer can be executed. This would help ensure that the land being transferred is accurately described and that there are no errors or discrepancies in the records.

Another benefit of smart contracts is that they can be used to automate the resolution of disputes that may arise between parties involved in a land ownership transfer. For example, a smart contract could include a mechanism for resolving disputes through an automated arbitration process. This would help ensure that disputes are resolved quickly and fairly, without the need for costly and time-consuming legal battles.

It is important to note that while smart contracts can help mitigate the risks associated with fraud and manipulation, they are not foolproof. In order to be effective, smart contracts must be carefully designed, programmed, and audited to ensure that they function as intended. Furthermore, smart contracts cannot address all of the potential risks associated with blockchain-based land ownership systems, such as the risk of corrupt government officials manipulating the records. However, they can be a valuable tool for reducing the risk of fraud and manipulation and improving the overall efficiency and transparency of the land ownership transfer process.

Potential for corruption in land registration process

While blockchain technology has the potential to reduce corruption in land registration processes, it is not immune to it. In fact, some experts argue that the use of blockchain technology could even increase the risk of corruption in certain situations. Here are some potential ways in which corruption could occur:

1. Manipulation of data: Blockchain technology is designed to be immutable, meaning that once a record is added, it cannot be altered or deleted. However, this assumes that the data entered into the blockchain is accurate and honest. If corrupt actors are able to manipulate the data before it is added to the blockchain, they could potentially control the entire system.

2. Access to the system: Blockchain technology relies on a network of nodes to verify and confirm transactions. If a corrupt actor gains control of enough nodes, they could potentially manipulate the system to their advantage.

3. Discretionary power: In many countries, the land registration process involves a great deal of discretionary power on the part of government officials. This means that officials may have the power to alter land records or make decisions about land ownership based on personal biases or

bribes. Even if the blockchain system is secure, corrupt officials could still manipulate the process.

4. Lack of transparency: In some cases, the use of blockchain technology for land registration could actually reduce transparency and accountability. This could occur if the government or other entities involved in the land registration process do not provide sufficient access to the blockchain records or if the records are not adequately audited.

To address these potential risks, it is important to carefully consider the design and implementation of any blockchain-based land registration system. Transparency, accountability, and appropriate safeguards are essential to ensuring that the system is secure and trustworthy. Additionally, there may be a need for ongoing monitoring and auditing of the system to detect and address any potential issues that arise. Ultimately, the success of any blockchain-based land registration system will depend on the willingness and ability of all stakeholders to work together to create a fair and transparent system that serves the interests of all parties involved.

Manipulation by corrupt governments or land registry systems

One of the potential risks of using blockchain for land ownership documentation is the possibility of manipulation by corrupt governments or land registry systems. In many countries, land registry systems are under the control of the government or other centralized authorities, and this centralized control could be exploited to benefit certain individuals or organizations at the expense of others.

Corrupt officials could use their access to the land registry system to manipulate the records, alter ownership information, or forge land titles. This could result in illegal land grabbing, unfair distribution of land, or denial of land rights to rightful owners.

The use of blockchain technology for land ownership documentation could mitigate some of these risks by providing a transparent and secure system that is resistant to tampering. However, the risk of manipulation by those in control of the system still exists, and it is important to address these risks in the implementation of any blockchain system for land ownership documentation.

There are some potential strategies that could be employed to reduce the risk of manipulation. For example, implementing a multi-stakeholder governance structure for the blockchain system, where different stakeholders have a say in how the system is managed and operated, could reduce the risk of centralized control and manipulation. Additionally, ensuring that the land ownership data is open and accessible to the public, rather than being kept behind closed doors, could help prevent corruption and increase transparency.

Another strategy is to establish an independent audit mechanism to monitor the blockchain system and ensure that it is operating transparently and securely. This could involve regular audits of the blockchain system and its management, as well as audits of the land ownership data itself to identify any inconsistencies or errors.

Overall, the potential for manipulation by corrupt governments or land registry systems is a significant risk when using blockchain for land ownership documentation. However, there are strategies that can be employed to reduce this risk and ensure that the system operates transparently and fairly for all stakeholders involved.

Consequences of unfair land ownership distribution

In the context of land ownership documentation, unfair land ownership distribution can be a significant consequence of corruption in the land registration process. When corrupt officials or systems manipulate land ownership records, it can lead to a distribution of land that benefits certain individuals or organizations at the expense of others. This can have far-reaching and damaging consequences for society as a whole, particularly for marginalized groups and those with fewer resources.

One potential consequence of unfair land ownership distribution is the exacerbation of existing social and economic inequalities. If corrupt officials or systems prioritize certain individuals or organizations for land ownership, it can result in a concentration of wealth and power in the hands of a few, while others are left with limited opportunities and resources. This can lead to a sense of alienation and exclusion among those who feel they have been denied a fair chance at acquiring land.

In addition, unfair land ownership distribution can have negative impacts on the economy. When land ownership is concentrated in the hands of a few, it can limit the opportunities for small businesses and entrepreneurs to establish themselves and grow. This can stifle innovation and competition, ultimately leading to slower economic growth and fewer job opportunities.

Moreover, when certain groups are excluded from land ownership, it can have negative impacts on their overall well-being. Land ownership can provide a sense of security and stability, and can be a key factor in determining an individual's ability to access basic needs such as housing, food, and water. When individuals or groups are excluded from land ownership, they may be forced to live in unstable or unsafe conditions, which can lead to a host of negative health and social outcomes.

Finally, unfair land ownership distribution can have political consequences. When corrupt officials or systems manipulate land ownership records to benefit certain individuals or organizations, it can erode trust in government institutions and the rule of law. This can lead to a breakdown in social cohesion and stability, and can ultimately threaten the democratic process itself.

Given these potential consequences, it is important to carefully consider the risks of corruption in the land registration process, and to take steps to prevent it from occurring. Using blockchain technology can help mitigate these risks by providing a more secure and transparent system for land ownership documentation, reducing the potential for corruption and manipulation.

Blockchain solutions for corruption

Blockchain technology has the potential to mitigate corruption in the land ownership registration process. By providing a transparent and immutable ledger, blockchain can ensure that all transactions are recorded and that all parties have access to the same information.

One solution for reducing corruption is to use a permissioned blockchain, where only authorized parties are allowed to access the blockchain. This can help prevent unauthorized changes to records and reduce the risk of fraud and manipulation.

Another solution is to use smart contracts, which can automate the land ownership transfer process and ensure that it is carried out fairly and transparently. Smart contracts can be programmed to execute only when certain conditions are met, such as the completion of a sale or the transfer of ownership. This can help reduce the risk of corruption and ensure that all parties are treated fairly.

Moreover, the use of blockchain can also help to reduce the amount of paperwork involved in land ownership transfers, which can help to reduce opportunities for corruption. By providing a digital, tamper-proof record of all transactions, blockchain can also make it easier to track and trace the transfer of land ownership, thereby reducing the potential for corruption and fraud.

However, it is important to note that blockchain technology is not a panacea for corruption. While it can provide important tools for mitigating corruption, it cannot solve all of the underlying problems that lead to corruption in the land ownership registration process. For example, blockchain technology cannot address issues such as inadequate governance or lack of transparency in the land ownership registration process. Therefore, it is important to address these issues as well to ensure that the benefits of blockchain technology can be fully realized.

Chapter 3: Exclusion and Marginalization
Potential for exclusion of certain groups

While blockchain technology can offer benefits in terms of efficiency and security, it also has the potential to exclude certain groups from the land ownership documentation process. Some of the ways in which this exclusion could occur are:

1. Lack of access to technology: One of the main issues with using blockchain for land ownership documentation is that it requires access to technology, including internet access and devices such as smartphones or computers. This could exclude those who do not have access to such technology, either due to lack of infrastructure or financial constraints.

2. Limited understanding of technology: Even for those who have access to technology, there may be a lack of understanding of how to use blockchain and related technologies. This could result in exclusion for those who are not familiar with the technology, including the elderly or those in rural areas who may not have had exposure to such technology.

3. Language and cultural barriers: Another potential issue is the language and cultural barriers that may arise with the implementation of blockchain for land ownership

documentation. The technology and related documentation may be primarily in English or other languages that may not be familiar to certain groups, leading to exclusion and marginalization.

4. Lack of legal frameworks and regulations: The implementation of blockchain for land ownership documentation may require the development of legal frameworks and regulations that ensure fairness and prevent exclusion. However, in many countries, these frameworks may not exist or may be inadequate, leading to the potential for exclusion of certain groups.

It is important to address these issues in the implementation of blockchain for land ownership documentation to ensure that all groups have equal access and opportunities for ownership. Some potential solutions include:

1. Developing inclusive user interfaces and documentation: User interfaces and documentation should be developed in languages that are familiar to different groups, including indigenous languages. Additionally, the user interfaces should be intuitive and easy to use, even for those with limited technology experience.

2. Providing access to technology: Governments and organizations could provide access to technology, including

devices and internet access, to those who do not have it. This could include setting up computer centers in rural areas or providing subsidies for smartphones or other devices.

3. Addressing legal frameworks and regulations: Governments and organizations should work to develop legal frameworks and regulations that ensure fairness and prevent exclusion. This could include setting up dispute resolution mechanisms that are accessible to all, regardless of their financial or technological capabilities.

4. Community engagement and capacity building: Community engagement and capacity building could help to increase awareness and understanding of blockchain technology and its potential benefits for land ownership documentation. This could include holding workshops or training sessions in different languages or in culturally appropriate settings.

By addressing these issues and implementing solutions that ensure inclusivity, the potential for exclusion and marginalization can be minimized, and the benefits of blockchain technology for land ownership documentation can be fully realized.

Lack of access to technology

As noted in the introduction, one of the potential dark sides of using blockchain for land ownership documentation is the possibility of excluding certain groups, particularly those who do not have access to the technology. The lack of access to technology can be a significant barrier for many individuals, particularly in developing countries or in areas with limited infrastructure or resources.

In the context of land ownership documentation, the lack of access to technology could make it difficult for individuals to prove their ownership of land or to access information about land ownership. For example, if a blockchain system is used to record land ownership but individuals do not have access to the internet or other necessary technologies, they may not be able to verify their ownership of land or access information about the land registry.

Furthermore, the lack of access to technology could exacerbate existing inequalities in land ownership. Those who have access to the technology and are able to use it effectively may have an advantage in securing ownership of land or in resolving disputes, while those without access may be at a disadvantage. This could lead to further marginalization of certain groups, particularly those who are already vulnerable or disadvantaged.

It is important to consider how to address this potential issue in the implementation of any blockchain system for land ownership documentation. This could involve providing access to technology and resources to those who do not have it, as well as developing user-friendly interfaces and training materials to help individuals use the technology effectively. In addition, alternative methods of documentation and verification may be necessary for individuals who are unable to use blockchain technology.

In summary, the lack of access to technology is a potential risk of using blockchain for land ownership documentation, and steps should be taken to mitigate this risk and ensure that the benefits of the technology are accessible to all.

Marginalized groups negatively impacted

While blockchain technology has the potential to bring about greater transparency and efficiency in land ownership documentation, there are concerns that certain marginalized groups may be negatively impacted. These groups may include those who are not familiar with the technology or who do not have access to it, as well as those who have historically been excluded from land ownership.

One potential consequence of implementing blockchain for land ownership documentation is that it may exacerbate existing inequalities in land ownership. For example, in many developing countries, women and minority groups may not have the same legal rights to land ownership as men or members of the dominant ethnic group. If these groups do not have access to the technology or are not familiar with how to use it, they may be further marginalized in the land ownership process.

In addition, there are concerns that blockchain technology may not be inclusive of people with disabilities. For example, blind or visually impaired people may have difficulty accessing information that is presented solely in a visual format, while people with limited mobility may have difficulty using certain features of the technology.

Furthermore, it is possible that the implementation of blockchain for land ownership documentation could create new forms of exclusion. For example, if the technology is only available in certain languages, it could exclude those who do not speak those languages. Similarly, if the technology is only accessible through certain devices or internet connections, it could exclude those who cannot afford those devices or who live in areas with poor internet connectivity.

Overall, it is important to consider the potential impact on marginalized groups when implementing blockchain technology for land ownership documentation. Careful consideration should be given to ensuring that the technology is accessible and inclusive for all, and that it does not exacerbate existing inequalities. This may require additional resources and efforts to ensure that marginalized groups have access to the technology and are able to use it effectively.

Best practices for inclusivity and accessibility

While the use of blockchain technology in land ownership documentation has the potential to greatly benefit individuals and communities, it's important to consider the potential for exclusion and marginalization of certain groups. To ensure inclusivity and accessibility for all, there are several best practices that can be followed.

1. Engage and empower marginalized communities: The voices of marginalized communities must be heard in the development of blockchain solutions for land ownership documentation. Engage with these communities to identify their needs and ensure they have a say in the development process.

2. Develop user-friendly interfaces: Not everyone has the same level of technical knowledge or access to technology. To ensure inclusivity, user-friendly interfaces should be developed that are easy to understand and accessible to those with limited technical expertise.

3. Provide access to technology: As discussed earlier, lack of access to technology is a barrier to inclusivity. Efforts should be made to provide access to technology, such as providing access to public computers or mobile devices.

4. Consider cultural and linguistic diversity: Blockchain solutions should be designed to take into account

cultural and linguistic diversity, and provide information in multiple languages if necessary.

5. Ensure transparency: To build trust with communities, transparency is key. Ensure that blockchain solutions are transparent and provide clear information about the land ownership documentation process.

6. Develop community-based governance models: To ensure the needs of all members of a community are met, community-based governance models should be developed. This ensures that all stakeholders are involved in decision-making and are equally represented.

By following these best practices, the potential for exclusion and marginalization can be minimized, and the benefits of blockchain technology in land ownership documentation can be realized by all members of a community.

Potential for privacy violations

Introduction: As with any new technology, the use of blockchain for land ownership documentation raises concerns about potential privacy violations. The very nature of blockchain, which relies on a distributed ledger that is publicly accessible and tamper-proof, raises questions about the level of privacy that can be maintained.

Privacy risks of blockchain-based land ownership documentation:

1. Exposure of personal information: The use of blockchain technology for land ownership documentation could lead to the exposure of personal information, such as the identities of property owners, their contact information, and even their financial details. This could result in privacy violations, identity theft, and other related risks.

2. Data breaches: While blockchain technology is known for its security features, there is always a risk of data breaches. A security breach could result in unauthorized access to personal information, leading to privacy violations and other risks.

3. Lack of control over personal information: Since blockchain technology relies on a distributed ledger, once personal information is uploaded, it cannot be removed or

modified. This means that individuals have limited control over their personal information, which could lead to privacy violations.

Mitigating privacy risks:

1. Anonymity: One potential solution to privacy risks associated with blockchain technology is the use of anonymity. By using pseudonyms instead of real names, individuals can protect their identities and personal information.

2. Encryption: Encryption can be used to protect sensitive information that is uploaded to the blockchain. This can help prevent unauthorized access and data breaches.

3. Regulatory frameworks: Governments and other regulatory bodies can establish frameworks to protect privacy rights when it comes to blockchain-based land ownership documentation. These frameworks could include guidelines for the use of personal information and protocols for handling data breaches.

Conclusion: Privacy risks are a valid concern when it comes to the use of blockchain technology for land ownership documentation. However, by implementing best practices, such as anonymity and encryption, and establishing regulatory frameworks, these risks can be mitigated.

Personal information revealed in blockchain records

One of the key concerns around the use of blockchain technology for land ownership documentation is the potential for personal information to be revealed in the public blockchain records. Unlike traditional land registries, where personal information is typically kept confidential and only accessible to authorized individuals, blockchain records are designed to be transparent and publicly accessible.

This raises questions around data privacy and security, particularly for individuals who may be vulnerable to identity theft, fraud, or other forms of abuse. If personal information such as names, addresses, and other identifying details are included in the blockchain records, they could be easily accessible to anyone with access to the blockchain.

While some argue that this transparency could actually enhance privacy, by providing a more secure and tamper-proof record of ownership, others point out that it could expose individuals to a range of risks. For example, if a person's identity is linked to a specific property, they may become a target for criminals looking to steal their identity or commit other forms of fraud.

To address these concerns, some blockchain-based land ownership systems are exploring alternative ways of storing personal information. For example, some systems are using cryptography and other security measures to protect personal information, while others are exploring the use of off-chain storage solutions that allow for more flexible data privacy and control.

Ultimately, the success of blockchain-based land ownership systems will depend on their ability to balance the need for transparency with the need for privacy and security. By implementing strong data privacy and security measures, and by engaging with stakeholders to ensure that the system meets the needs of all users, blockchain could become a powerful tool for ensuring fair and transparent land ownership.

Identity theft and privacy violations

One of the major risks associated with the use of blockchain technology for land ownership documentation is the potential for identity theft and privacy violations. With the increased amount of personal information that can be stored on the blockchain, the risk of identity theft is higher than ever before.

Hackers may attempt to gain unauthorized access to personal information stored on the blockchain, such as names, addresses, and other sensitive details. Once this information is obtained, they may use it for fraudulent activities or sell it on the dark web to other cybercriminals.

Another potential privacy violation is the loss of anonymity that is often associated with blockchain technology. While the use of pseudonyms can help protect users' identities, it is not always foolproof, and it is possible for a user's identity to be revealed through other means. This loss of privacy can be particularly concerning for individuals who have legitimate reasons for keeping their identity private, such as victims of domestic violence or political dissidents.

Furthermore, if the blockchain is not designed to protect the privacy of its users, the data it contains can be misused by third parties. For instance, in a real estate transaction, the buyer and seller may not want their financial information made public, but this information could be exposed through the blockchain.

To mitigate the risk of identity theft and privacy violations, it is important to use secure blockchain networks with strong encryption and data protection measures. Additionally, users should be mindful of the personal information they provide and consider using pseudonyms or other techniques to protect their identities. Finally, government regulations may be needed to ensure that the privacy of individuals is protected in blockchain transactions.

Strategies for protecting privacy

Strategies for protecting privacy in blockchain-based land ownership documentation include a variety of technical and procedural solutions. These can help mitigate risks associated with the potential for personal information to be revealed in blockchain records, as well as reduce the likelihood of identity theft and other privacy violations.

One approach to protecting privacy is to use encryption techniques to secure the data stored on the blockchain. This can help ensure that sensitive personal information is not easily accessible to unauthorized parties. Additionally, access control mechanisms can be used to restrict who is able to view and modify the data on the blockchain, further reducing the risk of privacy violations.

Another strategy is to use a permissioned blockchain network, which restricts participation to trusted parties. This can help reduce the risk of unauthorized access and tampering, as well as limit the visibility of sensitive information to only those who have a legitimate need to know.

In addition to technical solutions, there are also procedural strategies that can be employed to protect privacy in blockchain-based land ownership documentation. For example, strong user authentication and identity verification protocols can help prevent impersonation and identity theft. Clear and comprehensive privacy policies can also be established to guide the collection, use, and disclosure of personal information, and to provide individuals with transparency and control over their data.

Ultimately, protecting privacy in blockchain-based land ownership documentation requires a multifaceted approach that combines technical and procedural solutions. By carefully considering the risks and implementing appropriate safeguards, it is possible to mitigate the potential for privacy violations and build trust in the use of blockchain technology for land ownership documentation.

Chapter 5: Accessibility

Importance of accessibility for everyone

The use of blockchain technology for land ownership documentation has the potential to bring significant benefits to society, including greater efficiency, security, and transparency in the land registration process. However, in order to fully realize these benefits, it is crucial that the technology is accessible to everyone, regardless of their background or circumstances. This means that the needs of all stakeholders must be considered and accommodated in the design and implementation of blockchain-based land registration systems.

One key reason why accessibility is important is that land is a vital resource for people all over the world, and secure land rights are essential for a range of purposes, including economic development, poverty reduction, and social stability. However, many people, particularly in developing countries, lack formal land titles or face barriers to accessing land registration services. Blockchain-based systems have the potential to overcome some of these barriers by providing a more efficient and transparent way of recording land ownership information, but only if the technology is designed with the needs of these populations in mind.

In addition to these broader social benefits, there are also practical reasons why accessibility is important for the success of blockchain-based land registration systems. For example, if certain stakeholders, such as marginalized groups or people with disabilities, are excluded from using the technology, it may undermine the accuracy and integrity of the land ownership records that are maintained on the blockchain. This could ultimately lead to legal disputes and challenges to the validity of the system as a whole.

Moreover, from an ethical standpoint, it is important that the benefits of blockchain technology are not restricted to a narrow group of individuals or organizations. As a decentralized and open system, blockchain has the potential to promote greater equity and inclusivity in a range of industries and sectors. By ensuring that land registration systems based on blockchain are accessible to all, we can help to ensure that this potential is fully realized.

To achieve this goal, it is important that accessibility is considered throughout the entire process of designing and implementing blockchain-based land registration systems. This includes everything from the choice of blockchain platform and smart contract design to the user interface and support services provided to stakeholders. By taking a holistic and user-centered approach, we can create systems that are more inclusive, transparent, and equitable, and that can help to bring the benefits of blockchain technology to everyone, regardless of their background or circumstances.

Accessibility issues that could arise

In the context of land ownership documentation, accessibility refers to the ability of all individuals, regardless of their socioeconomic status, geographic location, and physical abilities, to access and utilize land registration and management systems. While blockchain technology has the potential to improve accessibility, certain issues could arise that may further marginalize some groups. In this section, we will explore some of the accessibility issues that could arise when implementing blockchain technology for land ownership documentation.

1. Limited Internet access: A significant issue that could limit accessibility is the limited access to the internet. While blockchain technology can enable individuals to access land records from anywhere in the world, this benefit is only applicable to those with reliable and consistent internet access. Unfortunately, many individuals in rural or remote areas may lack access to the internet, which could lead to their exclusion from the system.

2. Limited technological literacy: While blockchain technology has the potential to simplify land ownership documentation processes, it is only beneficial if individuals are capable of utilizing the system. Limited technological literacy among the population could lead to the

underutilization of the system, which could further marginalize individuals without the resources or ability to use the technology effectively.

3. Limited language support: As blockchain technology is a global system, it is essential to ensure that it supports multiple languages. Lack of language support could lead to individuals being unable to utilize the system effectively, particularly if they are not fluent in the primary language used in the system.

4. Lack of physical accessibility: Individuals with disabilities may face difficulties accessing land registry offices or utilizing blockchain systems due to the lack of physical accessibility. Blockchain systems must be designed with accessibility in mind, such as incorporating text-to-speech or other assistive technologies.

5. High implementation costs: The implementation of blockchain systems can be costly, which could limit accessibility for low-income individuals and communities. The high cost of implementation could lead to further marginalization of low-income communities, perpetuating the existing inequalities in land ownership.

6. Lack of trust in the system: Individuals may be hesitant to use blockchain systems if they lack trust in the technology or the entities responsible for maintaining the

system. Lack of trust could limit accessibility to the system, as individuals may choose to continue utilizing traditional land ownership documentation methods.

7. Exclusion of informal landowners: Blockchain systems could potentially exclude informal landowners who lack formal documentation of their land ownership. Without a formal land ownership record, individuals may be unable to utilize blockchain systems, leading to their further marginalization.

In conclusion, the implementation of blockchain technology for land ownership documentation has the potential to improve accessibility. However, certain issues must be addressed to ensure that the technology is accessible to all individuals, including those in remote areas, low-income communities, and those with disabilities. Strategies to improve accessibility include investing in internet infrastructure, providing education and training programs for technological literacy, ensuring language support, designing systems with physical accessibility in mind, reducing implementation costs, and building trust in the technology and entities responsible for maintaining the system.

Blockchain solutions for refugees and vulnerable populations

Blockchain technology has the potential to help refugees and other vulnerable populations gain access to secure and reliable land ownership documentation, providing a level of stability and security that may be difficult to achieve through traditional means. The technology offers several unique benefits that can address some of the challenges faced by these populations.

One of the primary challenges for refugees is establishing their identity and documentation to support their legal right to land ownership. In many cases, refugees are unable to produce the necessary documentation to prove their ownership, and their rights to the property may be disputed. Blockchain technology offers a solution to this problem by providing a secure and tamper-proof record of ownership that is accessible to all parties involved in the transaction.

In addition to providing a secure record of ownership, blockchain can also help address the issue of corruption that is prevalent in many refugee and vulnerable populations. By using a decentralized ledger system, the potential for corruption and manipulation is significantly reduced, as all parties have access to the same information, and any attempt to tamper with the system will be detected and prevented.

Another key advantage of blockchain is its ability to facilitate micropayments, which can be particularly beneficial for refugees and other vulnerable populations. In many cases, these populations may not have access to traditional banking services or may be unable to make large upfront payments for land ownership. With blockchain technology, payments can be made in small increments, reducing the financial burden and making land ownership more accessible.

Several organizations are already exploring the use of blockchain technology to provide land ownership documentation to refugees and other vulnerable populations. For example, the United Nations Development Program (UNDP) is working with the government of Moldova to implement a blockchain-based land registry system that will provide more secure and reliable documentation for landowners. The system will also use smart contracts to automate the land transfer process, reducing the potential for corruption and manipulation.

Another example is the work being done by Bitland, a blockchain-based land registry system that aims to provide secure and reliable documentation for landowners in Ghana.

The system is particularly beneficial for rural landowners who may not have access to traditional documentation and legal services.

In conclusion, blockchain technology offers a promising solution to the challenges faced by refugees and other vulnerable populations when it comes to land ownership documentation. By providing a secure and tamper-proof record of ownership, reducing the potential for corruption and manipulation, and facilitating micropayments, blockchain can help make land ownership more accessible and secure for these populations. As the technology continues to evolve, we can expect to see more innovative solutions emerge that can help address the unique needs of these communities.

Case studies of successful projects

In this chapter, we will explore the importance of accessibility in land ownership documentation and how blockchain technology can help improve accessibility for all individuals. We will discuss the potential accessibility issues that could arise and highlight blockchain solutions for refugees and vulnerable populations. Additionally, we will provide case studies of successful projects that have implemented blockchain technology to increase accessibility.

Importance of accessibility for everyone

Accessibility refers to the ease of use and access to information or services for all individuals, regardless of their physical or mental abilities, language proficiency, or socio-economic status. It is an important aspect of ensuring equal access to resources and services, including land ownership documentation.

In many countries, particularly developing countries, there are significant accessibility challenges that affect access to land ownership documentation. These challenges include language barriers, low literacy rates, inadequate infrastructure, and limited resources. Such challenges disproportionately affect marginalized groups, including refugees, indigenous peoples, and individuals living in poverty.

Blockchain technology has the potential to address some of these accessibility issues and promote greater inclusivity in land ownership documentation systems.

Accessibility issues that could arise

While blockchain technology can improve accessibility, it can also create new accessibility challenges. For example, the use of smartphones or computers for accessing blockchain-based land ownership documentation systems may exclude individuals who do not have access to technology or lack the necessary digital skills to use these tools.

In addition, the use of blockchain technology may require internet connectivity, which could be limited or unreliable in certain regions. This could limit access to the land ownership documentation system and hinder the ability of individuals to assert their property rights.

Furthermore, the use of blockchain technology could exacerbate existing power imbalances and socio-economic disparities. For example, individuals who lack the financial resources or technical knowledge to participate in the blockchain-based land ownership system may be excluded from the benefits of the technology.

Blockchain solutions for refugees and vulnerable populations

Blockchain technology can provide solutions to some of the accessibility challenges faced by refugees and vulnerable populations in accessing land ownership documentation. For example, blockchain can provide secure and tamper-proof land ownership records that are easily accessible through a digital platform. This eliminates the need for physical documents, which may be lost, stolen, or destroyed.

Additionally, blockchain technology can enable the creation of self-sovereign identities for refugees and vulnerable populations, which can help them establish legal identities and assert their property rights. Self-sovereign identities are digital identities that are controlled by individuals, not centralized institutions. These identities can be used to verify an individual's identity, and can help refugees and vulnerable populations establish their legal identity even if they lack the necessary government-issued identification documents.

Case studies of successful projects

There are several successful projects that have implemented blockchain technology to increase accessibility to land ownership documentation for refugees and vulnerable populations.

One such project is Bitland, a Ghana-based blockchain company that is using blockchain technology to create secure land title deeds for individuals in rural areas of Ghana. The company uses blockchain technology to create a tamper-proof, immutable record of land ownership, which can be easily accessed through a digital platform. The platform enables individuals to register their land ownership and establish legal ownership of their property.

Another successful project is the UN World Food Programme's Building Blocks project, which is using blockchain technology to provide food assistance to refugees in Jordan. The project uses blockchain technology to create a digital record of transactions, which enables refugees to purchase food at local markets using a digital wallet. The use of blockchain technology has made the process more efficient and secure, and has reduced the risk of fraud and corruption.

*****

In conclusion, accessibility is an important aspect of ensuring equal access to resources and services, including land ownership documentation. While blockchain technology has the potential to address some of the accessibility challenges faced by refugees and vulnerable populations, it can also create new accessibility challenges. It is important to carefully consider the potential

Chapter 6: Governance
Governance issues with blockchain-based land ownership documentation

Blockchain-based land ownership documentation offers many advantages, but there are also several governance issues that must be addressed. The decentralization and transparency of blockchain can present challenges for effective governance, as well as legal and regulatory frameworks.

One of the main governance issues is related to the verification of identity and ownership. In a decentralized system, there may not be a centralized authority that can effectively verify the identity of users and their ownership of land. This can lead to disputes and legal issues, as well as concerns about fraud and manipulation.

Another challenge is the need for clear legal and regulatory frameworks that can guide the use of blockchain-based land ownership documentation. These frameworks must address issues such as property rights, land use, and environmental protection. They must also be able to adapt to the rapidly evolving technology of blockchain, which can be challenging for traditional legal and regulatory frameworks.

Another potential governance issue is the risk of capture by powerful interests. Decentralized systems can be vulnerable to capture by individuals or groups with significant resources or influence, which can lead to the concentration of power and influence within the system. This can undermine the transparency and fairness of the system, and lead to further exclusion and marginalization.

Finally, there is the issue of scalability. As the use of blockchain-based land ownership documentation grows, it may become more difficult to manage and govern the system effectively. This can lead to issues such as reduced transparency and accountability, as well as increased vulnerability to fraud and manipulation.

To address these governance issues, it is important to develop clear legal and regulatory frameworks that can guide the use of blockchain-based land ownership documentation. These frameworks should be flexible enough to adapt to the rapidly evolving technology of blockchain, while also providing clear guidance on issues such as property rights, land use, and environmental protection.

It is also important to develop effective mechanisms for identity verification and ownership verification within the blockchain system. This may involve the development of new technologies and protocols, as well as the establishment of new governance structures that can provide oversight and accountability.

To address the risk of capture by powerful interests, it may be necessary to develop mechanisms for distributed decision-making and governance. This can involve the use of smart contracts and other decentralized governance structures that can help to ensure transparency and fairness in decision-making.

Finally, to address issues of scalability, it may be necessary to develop new technologies and protocols that can help to manage and govern blockchain-based land ownership documentation systems at scale. This may involve the development of new consensus mechanisms, as well as the use of off-chain scaling solutions.

In conclusion, governance issues present a significant challenge for the use of blockchain-based land ownership documentation. To address these issues, it is important to develop clear legal and regulatory frameworks, effective mechanisms for identity and ownership verification, distributed decision-making and governance mechanisms, and new technologies and protocols that can help to manage and govern blockchain-based land ownership documentation systems at scale.

Questions to ensure proper governance

As with any technology, the implementation of blockchain-based land ownership documentation requires proper governance to ensure its success. Governance refers to the processes and structures used to make decisions, allocate resources, and manage risks. Without effective governance, blockchain-based land registration systems may face challenges that could lead to their failure.

There are several questions that stakeholders should consider when developing governance structures for blockchain-based land ownership documentation:

1. Who are the stakeholders and what are their roles and responsibilities? It is important to identify all stakeholders involved in the implementation of blockchain-based land registration systems, including government agencies, landowners, technology providers, and civil society organizations. Each stakeholder has a role to play in the governance of the system, and their responsibilities should be clearly defined.

2. How will decisions be made? The decision-making process should be transparent, and all stakeholders should have an opportunity to participate. The process should also be based on clear and consistent criteria to ensure fairness and equity.

3. How will disputes be resolved? Disputes are inevitable, and there needs to be a mechanism in place for resolving them. The mechanism should be fair, transparent, and accessible to all stakeholders.

4. What are the risks and how will they be managed? There are several risks associated with blockchain-based land registration systems, including technical failures, security breaches, and governance failures. Risk management strategies should be developed to mitigate these risks.

5. How will data be protected and managed? Data protection is critical for the success of blockchain-based land registration systems. There should be clear policies and procedures for data protection and management, including data privacy and security.

6. How will the system be monitored and evaluated? Monitoring and evaluation are critical for assessing the effectiveness of blockchain-based land registration systems. There should be clear metrics for measuring the success of the system, and regular evaluations should be conducted to identify areas for improvement.

Proper governance structures can help ensure the success of blockchain-based land ownership documentation systems. By considering these questions, stakeholders can develop effective governance structures that promote transparency, fairness, and accountability.

Promoting transparency and accountability

Blockchain technology has the potential to improve transparency and accountability in governance, including in the context of land ownership documentation. By providing an immutable and transparent ledger, blockchain can help ensure that records and transactions are open and trustworthy, and that corruption and fraud are minimized. However, as with any technology, there are challenges and limitations to consider.

One challenge is the need to balance transparency with privacy. While blockchain can offer improved transparency, it must also respect individual privacy and data protection. In the context of land ownership, this means ensuring that personal information is kept secure, and that only authorized parties have access to sensitive information. It may also involve implementing privacy-enhancing technologies, such as zero-knowledge proofs or differential privacy, to ensure that individuals' data is protected while still allowing for transparency.

Another challenge is ensuring that the governance of blockchain-based land ownership systems is robust and effective. This may involve establishing clear governance structures, including roles and responsibilities for different stakeholders, and ensuring that these structures are transparent and accountable. It may also involve implementing mechanisms for resolving disputes and ensuring that all parties have access to the system on equal terms.

To promote transparency and accountability in blockchain-based land ownership documentation, there are several strategies that can be employed. These include:

1. Open standards and interoperability: By establishing open standards for blockchain-based land ownership documentation, it becomes easier for different systems to work together, and for different stakeholders to access and use the system. This can help ensure that the system is transparent and inclusive, and that all parties have equal access to the benefits of the technology.

2. Decentralized governance: By decentralizing governance of the system, it becomes more transparent and accountable. This may involve creating a decentralized autonomous organization (DAO) to govern the system, or using other mechanisms that ensure that all parties have a say in the governance of the system.

3. Auditability and accountability: By ensuring that all transactions on the blockchain are auditable, it becomes easier to hold parties accountable for their actions. This can be done through various means, such as using smart

contracts that execute automatically when certain conditions are met, or through mechanisms for resolving disputes.

4. Education and outreach: By educating stakeholders on the benefits and limitations of blockchain-based land ownership documentation, it becomes easier to build trust and ensure that the system is used effectively. This may involve providing training on how to use the system, or developing educational materials that explain the benefits and limitations of the technology.

5. Ethical considerations: By considering ethical issues from the outset, it becomes easier to design systems that promote transparency and accountability. This may involve conducting an ethical impact assessment, or establishing ethical guidelines for the use of the technology. It may also involve ensuring that the system is designed to benefit all stakeholders, including marginalized and vulnerable populations.

Case studies can also provide useful insights into how transparency and accountability can be promoted in blockchain-based land ownership documentation. For example, in Sweden, the Lantmäteriet land registry has been exploring the use of blockchain to improve the transparency and efficiency of its land registration system. By using a private blockchain, Lantmäteriet has been able to reduce the time required for property transactions and ensure that records are accurate and tamper-proof.

Another example is the Bitland project in Ghana, which uses blockchain technology to help resolve land disputes and promote transparency in land ownership. By creating a decentralized land registry, Bitland has been able to provide an accessible and transparent system for land ownership documentation, and has helped resolve disputes that were previously difficult to resolve through traditional means.

*****

In conclusion, promoting transparency and accountability in blockchain-based land ownership documentation is essential to ensuring that the technology is used effectively and to the benefit of all stakeholders. By considering issues such as privacy, governance, auditability, education, and ethics, it becomes possible to design systems that promote fairness, security, and accessibility. However, achieving effective governance of blockchain-based land ownership documentation requires more than just technology. It also requires trust, collaboration, and participation from all stakeholders. Ultimately, it is only through a concerted effort to address governance challenges that blockchain-based land ownership documentation can achieve its full potential as a tool for promoting social and economic development.

Blockchain technology has the potential to transform land ownership documentation by increasing transparency, security, and efficiency. In this section, we will examine some case studies of successful projects that have implemented blockchain-based land registry systems and the lessons that can be learned from them.

1. Sweden's Land Registry System Sweden is considered one of the pioneers of using blockchain technology in land registration. In 2016, the Swedish Land Registry began testing blockchain technology for property transactions. The project aimed to streamline the land registration process and reduce fraud by providing a secure and tamper-proof database. The Swedish Land Registry's blockchain system has been successfully tested with real estate transactions, and the government plans to expand the system to cover more areas in the future. The project's success can be attributed to its strong focus on governance and transparency, with a clear process for recording and validating transactions.

2. The Republic of Georgia's Land Registry System The Republic of Georgia has implemented a blockchain-based land registry system that has made the process of land registration more efficient, transparent, and secure. The

project was launched in 2017 and has successfully registered more than 1.5 million land titles. The system provides real-time updates on land registration and allows users to verify the authenticity of land titles. The project's success can be attributed to the government's commitment to the project, with the Prime Minister taking an active role in promoting the project.

3. Bitfury's Blockchain-Based Land Registry System in Ukraine Bitfury, a blockchain technology company, has collaborated with the government of Ukraine to develop a blockchain-based land registry system. The system aims to reduce corruption and streamline the land registration process. The project has been piloted in several regions of Ukraine and has shown promising results, with land registration times reduced from weeks to hours. The project's success can be attributed to its strong governance and collaboration between the government and the private sector.

4. The United Arab Emirates' Blockchain-Based Land Registry System The Dubai Land Department (DLD) has launched a blockchain-based land registry system that aims to increase transparency and reduce the time and cost associated with land registration. The project uses smart contracts to automate the land registration process, reducing

the need for intermediaries and increasing the speed of the process. The system has been successfully piloted, with more than 40 government entities and private companies participating. The project's success can be attributed to the DLD's strong governance and commitment to innovation.

These case studies demonstrate that successful blockchain-based land registry systems require strong governance, transparency, and collaboration between the public and private sectors. The projects that have been successful have clear processes for recording and validating transactions, and a commitment to promoting transparency and accountability. The use of smart contracts and automation has also been key to the success of these projects, reducing the need for intermediaries and increasing the speed and efficiency of the land registration process.

Conclusion
Recap of potential risks

Blockchain technology holds significant potential to transform land ownership documentation, creating a more efficient, transparent, and secure system that benefits all stakeholders. However, like any new technology, blockchain is not without risks. Over the course of this book, we have explored several potential risks associated with the use of blockchain for land ownership documentation. In this chapter, we will provide a recap of those risks and consider what steps can be taken to mitigate them.

Fraud and Manipulation One of the most significant risks associated with blockchain-based land ownership documentation is fraud and manipulation. The use of smart contracts and other blockchain-based tools can help mitigate this risk, but it is essential to design systems that take into account the potential for fraud and manipulation.

Corruption Corruption is another potential risk associated with the use of blockchain for land ownership documentation. The potential for corruption exists both in the land registration process and through manipulation by corrupt governments or land registry systems. However, blockchain technology can help to mitigate these risks by providing transparency and accountability and ensuring that ownership records cannot be altered or manipulated.

Exclusion and Marginalization The use of blockchain for land ownership documentation could potentially exclude certain groups, particularly those who lack access to technology or who may be negatively impacted by the distribution of land ownership. To address this risk, it is essential to consider best practices for inclusivity and accessibility, including ensuring that systems are designed with marginalized populations in mind.

Privacy Privacy is another significant risk associated with the use of blockchain for land ownership documentation. The use of blockchain can reveal personal information in blockchain records, potentially leading to identity theft and other privacy violations. However, there are strategies for protecting privacy, including designing systems that prioritize anonymity, data minimization, and user control.

Accessibility The use of blockchain for land ownership documentation could also create accessibility issues, particularly for vulnerable populations like refugees. Blockchain technology can help to mitigate these risks by providing secure and accessible systems for storing and sharing land ownership records.

Governance Finally, governance issues with blockchain-based land ownership documentation are another potential risk. To ensure proper governance, it is essential to consider questions of transparency, accountability, education, and ethics when designing blockchain-based land ownership systems.

Mitigating Risks To mitigate the risks associated with blockchain-based land ownership documentation, it is essential to design systems that take into account the potential for fraud, corruption, exclusion, privacy violations, and governance issues. This can be achieved through a range of strategies, including the use of smart contracts, privacy-enhancing technologies, and robust governance frameworks.

Conclusion Blockchain technology holds enormous potential to transform land ownership documentation, creating a more efficient, transparent, and secure system that benefits all stakeholders. However, it is important to acknowledge and address the potential risks associated with this new technology. By designing systems that prioritize transparency, accountability, inclusivity, and privacy, it is possible to create blockchain-based land ownership systems that work for everyone.

Call to action for responsible implementation

Blockchain technology has the potential to transform land ownership documentation and revolutionize the way we manage land records. However, as we have seen throughout this paper, there are potential risks and challenges associated with blockchain-based land registration, including corruption, exclusion, privacy violations, and governance issues.

To ensure the responsible implementation of blockchain-based land ownership documentation, there is a need for a collective call to action. All stakeholders, including government agencies, private sector entities, civil society organizations, and the international community, have a role to play in promoting responsible implementation.

One critical step is to ensure that blockchain-based land registration systems are designed with inclusivity and accessibility in mind. This means that systems must be designed in a way that ensures all stakeholders have equal access and that marginalized groups are not left behind. Governments and international organizations can provide support to ensure that the necessary infrastructure and technology are in place to promote inclusivity and accessibility.

Another key step is to ensure that blockchain-based land registration systems are transparent, accountable, and governed by ethical principles. Governments and international organizations should take the lead in promoting transparency and accountability by ensuring that blockchain-based systems are subject to appropriate regulatory oversight and that all stakeholders have access to information about how these systems work.

In addition, it is critical to ensure that blockchain-based land registration systems are designed in a way that promotes privacy and protects personal information. This requires that appropriate safeguards be put in place to ensure that sensitive data is not vulnerable to theft, hacking, or unauthorized access. Governments and international organizations can play a critical role in promoting privacy by developing appropriate data protection policies and regulations.

Finally, it is essential to promote education and awareness among all stakeholders about the benefits and risks of blockchain-based land registration systems. This includes providing education and training to government officials, private sector entities, and civil society organizations on how to design, implement, and govern blockchain-based systems.

In conclusion, the responsible implementation of blockchain-based land ownership documentation is critical to ensure that the potential benefits of this technology are fully realized and that the risks and challenges are effectively managed. This requires a collaborative effort by all stakeholders to ensure that systems are designed in a way that promotes inclusivity, accessibility, transparency, accountability, privacy, and ethical governance. By taking a proactive and responsible approach to the implementation of blockchain-based land registration, we can help to promote sustainable and equitable land management practices that benefit all stakeholders.

Recommendations for inclusive implementation

Chapter 1 of this report introduced blockchain technology and its potential application in land ownership documentation. Chapter 2 discussed the potential risks and challenges that could arise from implementing such a system, including corruption, unfair land ownership distribution, and the need for reliable data sources. Chapter 3 discussed the potential exclusion of certain groups, including those with limited access to technology, and the negative impact on marginalized populations. Chapter 4 highlighted potential privacy violations that could occur, including the revelation of personal information in blockchain records and identity theft. Chapter 5 examined accessibility issues and opportunities for blockchain solutions for refugees and vulnerable populations. Chapter 6 focused on governance issues, including the need for transparency and accountability, and featured case studies of successful projects.

Given the potential risks and challenges associated with implementing blockchain-based land ownership documentation, it is essential to take a responsible and inclusive approach to implementation. This requires a multi-stakeholder approach, including input from government officials, civil society organizations, and private sector actors.

Below are some recommendations for ensuring that the implementation of blockchain-based land ownership documentation is inclusive and equitable:

1. Engage in multi-stakeholder consultations: Governments and other stakeholders should engage in consultations with all affected groups to ensure that their voices are heard and their concerns are addressed.

2. Build in privacy protections: Privacy protections should be built into the design of any blockchain-based land ownership documentation system. This includes mechanisms for individuals to control their own data and ensure that it is not disclosed without their consent.

3. Ensure data accuracy and reliability: Blockchain-based land ownership documentation systems depend on accurate and reliable data sources. Governments and other stakeholders should invest in building and maintaining reliable data sources to ensure the integrity of the system.

4. Promote inclusivity: Efforts should be made to ensure that the system is accessible to all, including those with limited access to technology or financial resources.

5. Ensure transparency and accountability: Governance structures should be designed to promote transparency and accountability, with clear lines of responsibility and mechanisms for oversight and monitoring.

6. Promote education and awareness: It is important to educate all stakeholders about the benefits and risks associated with blockchain-based land ownership documentation systems. This will help to ensure that all stakeholders are informed and can make informed decisions about their participation in the system.

7. Support ethical design: The design of blockchain-based land ownership documentation systems should be guided by ethical principles that prioritize the well-being of all stakeholders, rather than the interests of a particular group.

In conclusion, the implementation of blockchain-based land ownership documentation has the potential to revolutionize the way land ownership is documented and managed. However, to realize its potential, it is essential to take a responsible and inclusive approach to implementation. By engaging in multi-stakeholder consultations, building in privacy protections, ensuring data accuracy and reliability, promoting inclusivity, ensuring transparency and accountability, promoting education and awareness, and supporting ethical design, it is possible to ensure that the benefits of blockchain-based land ownership documentation are shared by all stakeholders.

Blockchain technology has enormous potential to transform the way we manage and transfer assets, including land. However, as we have seen, its implementation must be approached with care to ensure that it does not exacerbate existing societal inequalities or create new ones. As we move forward with the development and implementation of blockchain-based land ownership documentation, there are several areas where further research is needed to understand and address potential challenges and opportunities.

First, we need to develop a better understanding of the social, economic, and political factors that influence land ownership and tenure. Blockchain technology cannot solve all of the complex issues related to land governance and land rights, and it is essential to work with local communities and stakeholders to understand their needs and concerns. Participatory approaches that involve all relevant parties, including marginalized groups and vulnerable populations, can help ensure that blockchain solutions are tailored to local contexts and inclusive.

Second, we need to develop more sophisticated technical solutions that can address the privacy, security, and accessibility concerns associated with blockchain-based land ownership documentation. One promising approach is the use of privacy-enhancing technologies, such as zero-knowledge proofs or homomorphic encryption, which can protect the confidentiality of sensitive data while still enabling secure transactions. Additionally, blockchain solutions that are designed with accessibility in mind, such as those that can be accessed using basic mobile phones, can help ensure that the benefits of the technology are accessible to everyone.

Third, we need to continue to explore the potential for blockchain-based land ownership documentation to promote social and environmental sustainability. For example, blockchain solutions can be used to support community land trusts, which can help to prevent the concentration of land ownership in the hands of a few wealthy individuals and promote more equitable access to land. Blockchain can also be used to support the tracking of environmental data related to land use, such as carbon emissions, water usage, or soil quality, enabling more effective and transparent environmental management.

Finally, we need to ensure that the development and implementation of blockchain-based land ownership documentation is guided by ethical considerations. As with any technology, there is a risk that blockchain could be used to reinforce existing power structures or to undermine human rights. It is therefore essential that blockchain solutions are developed and implemented in a way that is guided by principles of equity, justice, and sustainability.

In conclusion, the development and implementation of blockchain-based land ownership documentation presents both opportunities and challenges. By working together to address the potential risks and by ensuring that the technology is implemented in an inclusive and ethical manner, we can leverage the power of blockchain to promote more equitable and sustainable land governance. Continued research and collaboration are essential to realizing this vision.

THE END

Potential References

Introduction:

Swan, M. (2015). Blockchain: Blueprint for a new economy. O'Reilly Media, Inc.

World Bank. (2020). "Land Administration and Management." Retrieved from https://www.worldbank.org/en/topic/land/administration

Chapter 1: Fraud and Manipulation

De Filippi, P., & Wright, A. (2018). Blockchain and the law: The rule of code. Harvard University Press.

Ong, J., & Wang, Q. (2020). "Blockchain and the future of real estate: A systematic review." Journal of Real Estate Literature, 28(2), 165-188.

Chapter 2: Corruption

Al-Ubaydli, O., & Fong, C. M. (2019). "Blockchain government-a next form of infrastructure." Journal of Public Policy, 39(1), 48-64.

Farooq, M., Tariq, A., & Ullah, A. (2018). "Land registration using blockchain technology." 2018 15th International Bhurban Conference on Applied Sciences and Technology (IBCAST), 621-626.

Chapter 3: Exclusion and Marginalization

Bass, L., & Dang, Q. V. (2018). "Blockchain and distributed ledger technologies for social impact: A review of challenges and opportunities." The Journal of Alternative Investments, 21(3), 67-83.

Hosseini, M., & Tonelli, R. (2018). "Can blockchain be the enabler of right to identity for refugees?." In International Conference on Human-Computer Interaction, 531-546. Springer, Cham.

Chapter 4: Privacy

Kosba, A., Miller, A., Shi, E., Wen, Z., & Papamanthou, C. (2016). "Hawk: The blockchain model of cryptography and privacy-preserving smart contracts." In 2016 IEEE Symposium on Security and Privacy (SP), 839-858.

Narayanan, A., Bonneau, J., Felten, E., Miller, A., & Goldfeder, S. (2016). "Bitcoin and Cryptocurrency Technologies: A Comprehensive Introduction." Princeton University Press.

Chapter 5: Accessibility

Heeks, R. (2017). "Understanding 'blockchain' technology: perspectives on potential challenges for development." Third World Quarterly, 38(8), 1710-1728.

Swan, M. (2015). Blockchain: Blueprint for a new economy. O'Reilly Media, Inc.

Chapter 6: Governance

Crosby, M., Pattanayak, P., Verma, S., & Kalyanaraman, V. (2016). "Blockchain technology: Beyond bitcoin." Applied Innovation, 2(6-10), 71-81.

Teegen, H., Doh, J. P., & Vachani, S. (2019). "Blockchain and its coming impact on higher education: Transforming the University." Journal of International Business Education, 14, 69-82.

Conclusion:

Buterin, V. (2014). "A next-generation smart contract and decentralized application platform." White Paper, Ethereum Project, 1-32.

Kshetri, N. (2018). "Blockchain's roles in meeting key supply chain management objectives." International Journal of Information Management, 39, 80-89.